C000270628

NOT
JUST...

HOLS

Not Just for Christmas

By
Mark Greenwood

Illustrated by
Andy S. Gray

revmarkgreenwood.com
Twitter @revgreenie

onegraydot.com
linkedin | instagram @onegraydot

Published for Mark Greenwood in 2023
by Verité CM Limited
www.veritecm.com

Proofread by Louise Stenhouse
louise.stenhouse@btinternet.com

ISBN: 978- 1 -914388-45-3

Typeset by Andy S. Gray, Onegraydot Ltd
Printed in England

Dedicated to my wife Emma,
and daughters
Robin and Nathalie,
for all the lovely celebrations of
Advent and Christmas
we've had together.

Contents

Have you done your
Christmas shopping yet?

What day is it?

If you're not good enough Santa won't come

The Christmas Number 1

Christmas trees

It's the must-have gift

What's your favourite
Christmas carol?

Awwww, you really shouldn't have

May I wish you a Merry Christmas

I absolutely love nativity plays. I was perhaps a little proud when my daughter played Mary – I mean we are talking about the mother of Jesus here! I have read some funny stories about nativities and this is one of my favourites.

To show the radiance of Jesus at a school Christmas play, the newly born Saviour was lit up by an electric light, which was hidden in the manger. All the stage lights were to be turned off so that only the brightness of the manger would be seen. When the moment arrived, the boy who was controlling the lights was suddenly struck with a sense of fear and confusion, resulting in him turning off all the lights, including the manger. A tense moment followed, which was relieved only by one of the shepherds shouting, "He's switched Jesus off!"

I love it, but it does make me think that so often we turn Jesus off when Christmas is over. We put him away with the decorations as if he is only for Christmas and not for life.

In 1978 the Dogs Trust (then known as the National Canine Defence League) was concerned as it became popular for people to give puppies to family and friends at Christmas, which sadly were abandoned very soon after. Clarissa Baldwin was tasked with creating a slogan to seek to bring change. "A dog is for life not just for Christmas" was released.

As you read this light-hearted book my hope is that you will begin to see that Jesus is for your life and not just for Christmas. We will have a look at some of the things that make Christmas and what they can show us about how Jesus wants to help us live life to the full. Then, at the end, you will be invited to consider making him part of your life. I wonder if you would come with me on a Christmas journey to living life!

Mark

It's beginning to look a lot like Christmas

Face it, you are singing it in your head right now, aren't you? Written in 1951 by Meredith Willson, the song was originally titled "It's Beginning to Look Like Christmas". It has been recorded by many artists, including Perry Como, Bing Crosby and, more recently, my personal favourite Michael Bublé. You've got to love a bit of Bublé at Christmas – I start The Bublé Christmas Build-up about October. Don't judge me!

The problem with starting to play Bublé as soon as I do (I still get very excited about Christmas) is that we can get too Christmassy too soon. To be fair, I also want to keep the decorations, the trees and the lights up as along as I can, so I don't think I've ever run out of Christmas cheer!

Are you feeling Christmassy yet? I wonder what sounds, smells and sights make it look or feel like Christmas for you? The John Lewis advert? The lights switch-on? The school nativity play? The office Christmas do? The *Radio* or *TV Times* on the shelves? Or the sound of Slade's "Merry Christmas Everybody" as Noddy declares,

"It's Chriiiistmaaaaaaaass!"?

As much as I love nearly everything about Christmas, it's something else that brings the excitement for me. Jesus is what makes Christmas complete because Jesus is what makes life complete for me. I know this sounds cheesy but I feel Christmassy all year round because I know Jesus is there all year round – through the good times and the bad.

Think about this: Could it be that all the celebrating we do at Christmas is simply due to the fact that a real person called Jesus came into our world? Maybe it's time to bring him into your world.

The Radio and TV Times

As much as I love digital reading, I still love getting and having a flick through the *Radio Times*. Maybe for you it's the *TV Times*. Ooo, I wonder what "excellent" TV is on offer over Christmas? It's definitely one of the simple things that makes it look a lot like Christmas. I genuinely look forward to seeing it on the shelves.

Am I just romanticising what is was like when I was younger or is this a "getting older" thing? Is my reminiscing delusional? It just seems that Christmas TV is not what it used to be! I don't really want to watch Christmas specials of all the programmes I don't watch throughout the year.

All that said, every year I still read through each day's viewing and mark-up what I want to watch, though in truth I very rarely consult it to view what I wanted to! And when I do rarely pick it up, I realise what I have forgotten. The truth is, once I have done the initial flick through

of the festive TV magazine, it ends up being nothing more than a Christmas table decoration. I suppose there is so much more choice to Christmas TV with the arrival of Netflix, Amazon

Prime, Sky Movies, etc. Lots of choice but I still end up disappointed.

Whether it's a streaming platform or a coffee, we do seem to have so much more choice than ever before, and yet often we are more disappointed than ever! Jesus helps us to make the right choices in our life when we make him the number one choice in our life – a choice that is not disappointing.

Think about this: Is it time for you to choose to follow Jesus and let following him inform all your choices? Could this be what will make sense of your life?

What's your favourite Christmas movie?

National Lampoon's Christmas Vacation, *Love Actually*, *The Holiday*, *Elf*, *Santa Claus the Movie* 1, 2 and 3, *It's a Wonderful Life* (I've tried to watch it, honest), *Arthur Christmas*, *The Grinch Who Stole Christmas*, *Jingle All the Way* and, I mean, is *Die Hard* even a Christmas movie? I can hear the shouts at the book now, or maybe you have even launched it across the room in anger!

I'm a big fan of Christmas movies. I think the most I have done in one day is five – I named it A Christmasfilmathon. Sometimes my girls and I have a secret early Christmas film-watching day whilst my wife is out of the house – and we love it. I prefer Christmas films to all the non-film Christmas TV viewing. I eagerly wait for new Christmas films to come onto my streaming platforms.

My favourite Christmas film is *The Muppet Christmas Carol.* I love Dickens' story of Scrooge anyway but introduce the Muppets into any film and I am in! Michael Caine is one of my favourite actors – has he ever used any other accent than cockney? I think he plays Scrooge so well. Even though it's a slapstick comedic retelling with the Muppets, it's such a beautiful message that comes alive.

Scrooge is confronted with the reality of his past, present and future, which all seems so depressing – and yet there is hope. The film ends with a changed person, who in turn goes and changes the lives of others, seeking amends for his past and, in particular, how his love of money affected the way he has treated people.

Jesus helps us face all our yesterdays, todays and tomorrows, whatever they contain. We do not need to fear the past, the present or the future as Jesus helps us to face them. Jesus not only changes us, he also uses us to change our world around us – now that's hope.

Think about this: Does your past, your present or your future have things that concern you? Do you need peace to face them? Could this be found in Jesus?

What are your plans for Christmas and New Year?

Part of the normal Christmas chat is to find out what people are doing for Christmas and New Year. I love hearing what people are planning. And for some it NEEDS planning as it's complicated to say the least. I need a lie down when I listen to some tell me what they are planning to fit in! Some of our plans are our choice and some plans are purely down to what is expected by family and friends.

I remember asking some friends what they were doing for Christmas. One said, "Sleeping and eating," another said, "I don't know, my wife hasn't told me yet," and another said, "Nothing."

We often make plans for Christmas and New Year with an anticipation of it being great and yet, so often, it can be an anti-climax.

More people sign up to gyms and weight-loss classes in the weeks after Christmas and New Year than at any other time of year. We can often be disappointed with the experiences we had or the outcomes of them and then we just want a detox, to get back to normal, or to have a reset for the year ahead.

We often choose to live life according to our plan. Sometimes we live according to a plan that has been forced upon us that would never have been our plan. Becoming a follower of Jesus – a Christian – is about understanding that we can live life with God and follow his good, pleasing and perfect plan for our lives. Though it's not always easy, it's definitely the best plan. Jesus makes it possible for us to know and follow God's plan.

Think about this: Are you planning your future? Is it time to bring God into the plans for your life? Could it be that this would bring you maximum fulfilment?

I've eaten too much

I think it would be fair to say that every Christmas I can be heard at least once (though probably more) saying the words, "Ooooo, I've eaten too much," accompanied by, "I am not doing that again." But guess what? I do. Sometimes I may also utter the words, "Do not let me do that again," as though it is someone else's fault. My biggest problem is, I like food!

I find that not only do I have a pudding belly, I also have a

cheeseboard belly, a mince pie belly, a nuts belly, a crisps belly, a Fox's chocolate biscuit belly (you know the ones covered in chocolate), last but not least of the bellies, a box of chocolates belly. Whilst these bellies have not been medically verified, they definitely exist!

I am not surprised we put on weight. The average person eats and drinks around 7,000 festive calories just on Christmas Day. Did you know the

average mince pie contains 180 calories? Don't worry, though, I have a solution: 45 minutes of continual hoovering will burn off each mince pie. Did you ALSO know that in 1650 mince pies were considered to be so over-indulgent that an act of parliament was passed authorising the imprisonment of anyone found guilty of eating one? Be careful – to the best of my research, that law has not yet be rescinded! It's still technically illegal.

Christmas isn't about putting on weight, it's about losing what weighs us down. We all have things that weigh us down – some due to our own decisions and some not – but, whatever they are, Jesus wants to help us with what weighs us down in life.

Think about this: What are the things that weigh you down and cause you concern? Is it time to give them to Jesus – to live free from them?

Have you done your Christmas shopping yet?

I don't think I have ever met anyone quite as on it when it comes to Christmas shopping as my mum. She not only buys enough food for Christmas but also to carry her well into the New Year. Seriously, you should see the stock of tins on the cellar-head shelves. It's like she's got some inside knowledge of a looming global disaster!

My wife is pretty good too as she buys the girls' presents throughout the year, sometimes even buying presents that she gives a few years after – now that's organised. I'm a little more last minute, if I am honest, and often haven't got any idea what to buy. I now have a list of desired items from the family. It's very helpful!

It has been estimated that the average family will spend £1,000 on top of their normal monthly budget. Fuel for visiting family members, the Christmas food and drink,

the must-have presents that you feel your children should have because their friends have them, and more. The pressure to spend at Christmas is massive.

I think we all spend money on things that don't bring any real satisfaction. They not only leave a deficit in our bank account, they can also leave a deficit in our lives. A famous credit card company's Christmas advertising slogan one year declared, "The good news this Christmas is that we have cut the interest on our card."

The good news this Christmas is the same good news as every Christmas and it has nothing to do with a credit card.
The good news is that instead of God punishing us for our wrong, Jesus took that for us. The cost of your forgiveness was the life of Jesus – he took it so you wouldn't have to. No cost was too great for God and no cost is too great for us when you understand what it cost God.

Think about this: What are the things you have done wrong in your life that you need God to forgive you for? Are there people that you need to forgive?

What day is it?

Do you find yourself asking other members of the family, "What day is it?" And quite frankly they are of no help, as they haven't got a clue either.

Christmas Eve, Christmas Day and Boxing Day are a blur, but New Year hasn't quite arrived. We've consumed food and drink in never-been-seen-before volumes. We have pulled our fair share of crackers, read the terrible jokes, solved

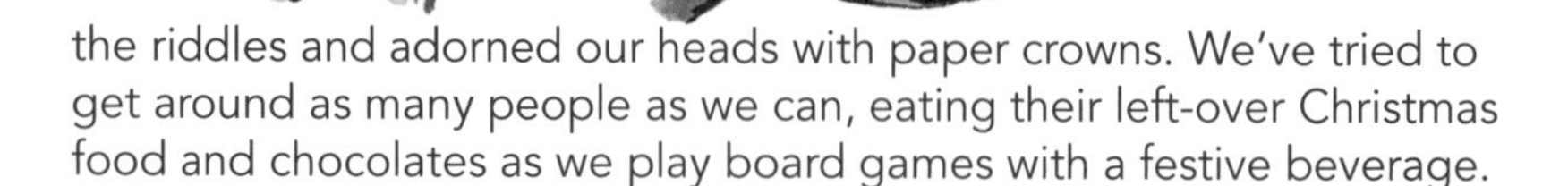

the riddles and adorned our heads with paper crowns. We've tried to get around as many people as we can, eating their left-over Christmas food and chocolates as we play board games with a festive beverage.

The result? We don't know where we are or what day it is. We are oblivious to what's happening around us as we have pulled away from the stress of everyday life. But we can find ourselves feeling a bit out of it.

So often life can feel like that. The routine and pressures of living in what seems to be a bad-news world and simply trying to get through each day, looking forward to the weekend and a chance to chill. We can sometimes feel a bit lost, or at least not quite sure of where we are going in life. We can sometimes wonder what life is all about and whether we can depend on anything.

When we think of Jesus at Christmas we often only see him just as a baby or even a lovely fairy tale for the kids. Even if we see him as a real person – an historical figure – who lived over 2,000 years ago and over 2,000 miles away, we don't see that he has any real relevance to our lives. And yet the reality is Jesus brings purpose and direction to our lives if we allow him. You only need to chat to one of over 2 billion people across the globe who are Christians and they will tell you that Jesus is not only the way to God, he's the way to life and living with purpose and direction. He is real and relevant.

Think about this: Do you find yourself wandering through life and wondering about life? Is it time to find real purpose and direction in Jesus?

If you're not good enough Santa won't come

Have you ever tried to make yourself sleep when you have got something happening the next day that is exciting, scary or sad? Maybe your mind is so full of stuff it won't switch off? Or that you have to get up extra early and you are nervous you may not hear your alarm?

It's on nights like these that you see nearly every hour pass – it can be so frustrating. Oh, the stress when I was young as my parents would say on Christmas Eve, "If you don't go to sleep Santa won't come." Or to add even more persuasion (or, as I like to call it, stress), "If you're not GOOD enough, Santa won't come"!

It was so difficult but I knew I needed to sleep on Christmas Eve or it was deemed not being good enough. Sometimes I was convinced I'd heard Santa's sleigh bells jingling! Christmas for me had become all about being good enough so that someone would come. The problem is – I knew I wasn't that good!

I now know that Christmas isn't about being good enough so someone will come. It's about the fact that we weren't good enough so someone had to come. When I look at my life there are things I think, say and do that I am not happy with, and so it comes as no surprise to me that there are things that God isn't happy with when he looks at my life.

At Christmas, I love the reminder that Jesus was called Jesus because that name means "he saves". In other words, he rescues us from the things we all think, all say and all do, forgiving us and giving us the desire and power to live differently. There is nothing that makes us good enough for God, but that's why Jesus came to us. It's brilliant.

Think about this: What are the things you have thought, said and done that you shouldn't have? What are the things you didn't think, say or do that you should have? Ask God's forgiveness.

The Christmas Number 1

Okay, please don't judge me (again). I may, or may not, have listened to Christmas songs in September! Whether it's Mariah singing, "All I want for Christmas is you", Mud singing, "It will be lonely this Christmas without you", or Elton reminding me to "step into Christmas", I love Christmas songs. There are some great modern ones, too, by Leona Lewis, Ariana Grande and Kelly Clarkson that have made their way onto my massive Christmas Spotify playlist.

When I was younger I remember the anticipation of the Christmas Number 1. It doesn't quite seem to be the same these days, although I did note the tension when Ladbaby got Number 1 for the fifth time, surpassing The Beatles. I think some "serious artists" were probably a bit annoyed but it was all good fun and for a good cause, which kind of goes with Christmas really.

I love singing along to the Christmas songs. When I say "singing", I've never been good at remembering lyrics so there tends to be a lot of what I like to call "freestyling". We have a little tradition in our house that we play "Driving Home for Christmas" only when I travel home from speaking at my last carol service of the year. The rush to press next on the playlist when it comes up before then . . . !

My friend Chris Eaton wrote a song for Cliff Richard that made the UK Christmas Number 1 in 1990, reminding us that Christmas is "Saviour's Day". Christmas really is about Jesus putting us first – being born to rescue and save us by sacrificing his life. We were God's number one priority even above the life of his own son. This is mind blowing and beautiful.

Think about this: Is it time to put God in first place in your life, to make him number one and to put him in the driving seat of your life?

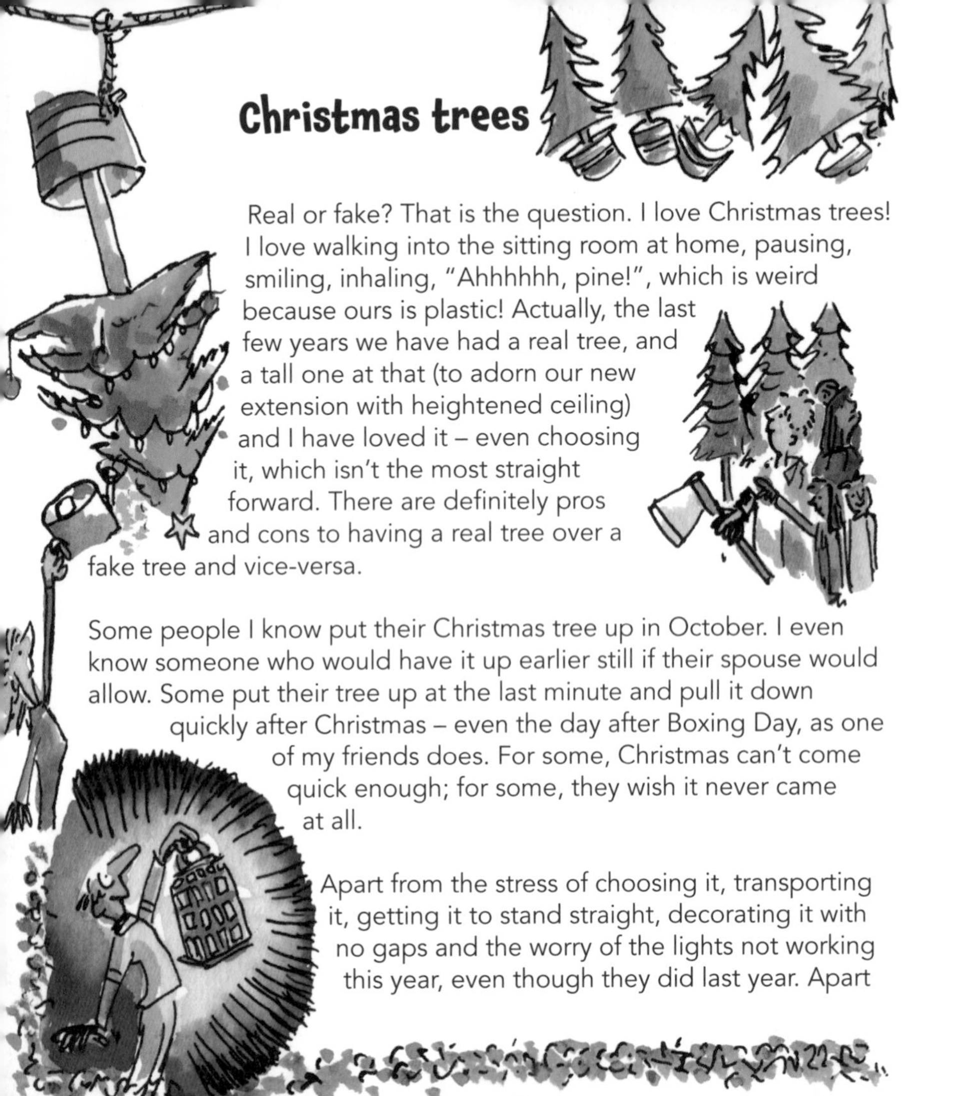

Christmas trees

Real or fake? That is the question. I love Christmas trees! I love walking into the sitting room at home, pausing, smiling, inhaling, "Ahhhhhh, pine!", which is weird because ours is plastic! Actually, the last few years we have had a real tree, and a tall one at that (to adorn our new extension with heightened ceiling) and I have loved it – even choosing it, which isn't the most straight forward. There are definitely pros and cons to having a real tree over a fake tree and vice-versa.

Some people I know put their Christmas tree up in October. I even know someone who would have it up earlier still if their spouse would allow. Some put their tree up at the last minute and pull it down quickly after Christmas – even the day after Boxing Day, as one of my friends does. For some, Christmas can't come quick enough; for some, they wish it never came at all.

Apart from the stress of choosing it, transporting it, getting it to stand straight, decorating it with no gaps and the worry of the lights not working this year, even though they did last year. Apart

from then the pulling down, the getting rid and the future risk of a hiding pine needle getting under your toe nail in August (this did actually happen to me) I love 'em – no, genuinely, I really do! I love it at night time when the house lighting is lowered and we switch the tree lights on. I could look at it for ages.

However, Christmas for me isn't just about lights on a tree; it's about the Light of the World on a tree. Jesus called himself "the Light of the World" because he brings light into our lives. In the Bible it says that Jesus was placed on a tree. It's what the cross was called. Jesus, the Light of the World, was placed on a tree to take the punishment for our wrong. In doing this the disconnect between humans and God was dealt with, meaning that God's light could flood into our lives and we, in turn, get to take his light to others. It really does light up your life when you connect with God.

Think about this: Are there areas in your life that you need God to flood with his light? Are there places where you need to take God's light into?

It's the must-have gift

There's lots of chat about the must-have gift – the one gift that will "make" Christmas. I have had some amazing gifts – not necessarily expensive either. I have to say, though, I have also had my fair share of should-never-have-had gifts, most of them from my mum.

I've had pairs of white acrylic sports socks complete with their own supply of static electricity. I've had matching talc and aftershave of every cheap kind, from Brut to Hi-Karate, Insignia to Old Spice, and all these at the age of 7 – Oooo they sting. I've had a handkerchief with my initial on it, although my mum must have been in a rush because she got me one with a W and not an M! I've even had the mustn't of all mustn't-haves: soap . . . on a rope!

It can be a bit pressurising choosing the right gift for a person. Equal only to the stress of when you receive a gift that you don't like and you feel duty bound to say, "Ooooo, just what I've always wanted," and let's face it – it isn't what you have

always wanted. Christmas is not just about gifts for people, as lovely as that is, it's about the gift of a person called Jesus. The Bible says, "For to us a child is born, to us a son is given."

Jesus' birth was predicted over 400 years before he came. Added to that, well over 300 prophecies were made in the oldest part of the Bible about his birth, life, death and resurrection, that were all fulfilled in this gift of Jesus. You might not feel that Jesus is "just what I've always wanted" but he is "just what you have always needed".

Jesus is the must-have gift for Christmas and life, and he is the gift that keeps on giving. Wrapped up in this amazing must-have gift of Jesus is everything that you need for life: peace, forgiveness, hope, new life and connection with God.

Think about this: Is it time to put to one side what you think you want out of life and to give space to Jesus who brings us what we really need in life?

What's your favourite Christmas carol?

I love singing Christmas carols. It's so hard to choose my favourite. When I do, and then hear someone else say theirs, I get favourite-Christmas-carol envy.

Here it is, my favourite Christmas carol . . . "Silent Night", "O Holy Night", "Joy to the World", "Once in Royal David's City", "While Shepherd's Watch" (particularly good fun when sung to the tune of "Ilkla Moor Baht'at"), "O Come, All Ye Faithful", "Hark! The Herald Angels Sing", "Away in a Manger", "O Little Town of Bethlehem", "Ding Dong Merrily on High" . . . I think you get the idea – I love them all.

Christmas carols are songs of hope, telling the great truths of what God is like, what he has done for us and how it is revealed in Jesus who came to earth, meaning that we can know those truths personally. When you look at the life of Jesus, he helps you to understand what God is like, what he wants to do for us, and carols articulate some of these beautiful truths. That's why I so often feel emotional when I sing them. As much as I love listening to others sing them, I love belting them out myself and, unlike the Christmas songs I mention elsewhere in the book, there is no freestyling here as I know them so well.

Okay, I am going to nail my Christmas carol colours to the mast. I love "In the Bleak Midwinter", which, let's face it, sounds depressing but I love the last verse:

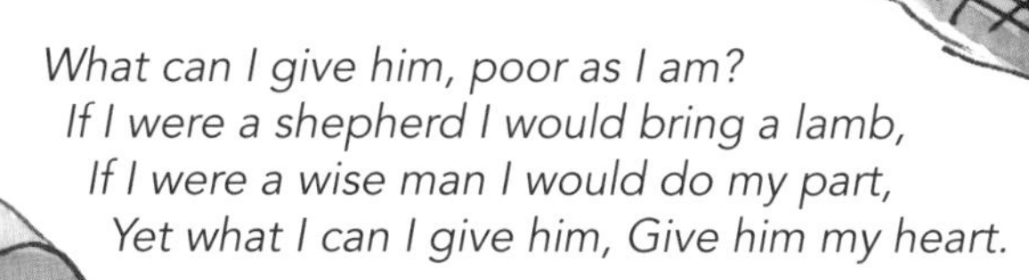

What can I give him, poor as I am?
If I were a shepherd I would bring a lamb,
If I were a wise man I would do my part,
Yet what I can I give him, Give him my heart.

It's a lovely truth that there is nothing we can give to God that will earn his love for us, but what he does ask for is our heart – our life. That does seem a lot but it pales into insignificance when you understand what he has done for us and what we get in return!

This Christmas why not give Jesus your heart and see the difference he makes in your life? Giving him your heart simply means you invite him into your life and your plans and seek, with his help, to live life his way and not yours. It starts by asking for his forgiveness and then you will begin to see that Jesus really is for life, and not just for Christmas.

Think about this: Is it time for you to invite Jesus into your life by giving him your heart – making him number one in your life? Over the next few pages you can read how you can do this.

Awwww, you really shouldn't have

I hope you have enjoyed reading *Not Just for Christmas.*

Christmas is a great time of year for a life reset and that's what this book is all about. Whoever you are, wherever you find yourself in life, Jesus is all about the reset. He really will detox and enrich your life if you let him.

Have you ever received a gift from someone and it has genuinely meant something that they thought of you? You've found yourself saying, "Awwww, you really shouldn't have," but actually you are glad that they did? Well, God has really thought about you and has given you something so precious, and today he is inviting you to receive it.

Big Yes

Many people have said a "Big Yes" to God, deciding to follow him and his ways. They have asked God to forgive them for leaving him out of their life and for doing their own thing. They have embraced Jesus' death on the cross and the fact that he came back to life. They have received his forgiveness and new life and joined with other believers in living for God and by making a difference in the world.

This Christmas, why don't you say a "Big Yes" to God now and receive all he has done for you and all he has for you? To do this, here are some words you can pray to God:

Dear God,

I have left you out of my life and done things wrong.
I ask for your forgiveness and thank you for sending your son Jesus to die for me.
Help me to turn away from life without you and now to live life with you.
Lead me in your ways that I might fully follow you.

Amen

If you said this and meant it, you are now connected with God and have started an exciting journey.

Little Yes

Some people aren't quite ready to say that "Big Yes" to God but they have made an intentional decision to find out more, to investigate whether Christianity is true and Jesus is who he says he is. This is what I call a "Little Yes". Sometimes it's because they are thinking about God and sometimes it's simply because they are thinking about life.

This Christmas would you be interested in finding out how you can investigate Christianity?

Healthy Maybe

Many people consider themselves open minded but don't always apply that to Christianity. A "Healthy Maybe" is someone who is willing to become open minded about Christianity or, if they are already open minded, they make a commitment to stay so and are maybe willing to chat about it openly.

This Christmas, would you be interested in becoming or staying open minded?

Yes Again

It might be that you are already a follower of Jesus but you know you have maybe wandered or slipped away a bit, or even wandered far away and you need to come back to God, or as my friend often says, "update your commitment to God".

This Christmas, do you need to say "Yes Again" to God?

If you are a Big Yes, Little Yes, Healthy Maybe or Yes Again, have a chat with whoever gave you this book so they can help you along your journey with Christ. If you don't have someone like that, connect with me at

revmarkgreenwood@gmail.com

I would love to help you on your journey.

Treat yourself this Christmas to a book that might be just what you have always needed

If you want to read more to help you with your response this Christmas, whether it's a **Big Yes, Little Yes, Healthy Maybe** or **Yes Again**, then why not visit my online shop.

Is it Possible . . . ?

is written to help you become open minded about God and the Christian faith, to help you become a **Healthy Maybe**.

Look Closer is written to help you investigate the basic message of Christianity, to become a **Little Yes**.

The Journey is written to help you if you have said a **"Big Yes"** to God or if you are very close to doing so. It's also helpful if you have said **"Yes Again"**.

Why not buy more copies of this book, or the books above, to give away? They may help many more people find that Jesus really is for life, not just for Christmas.

Available at **revmarkgreenwood.com**

HOLS